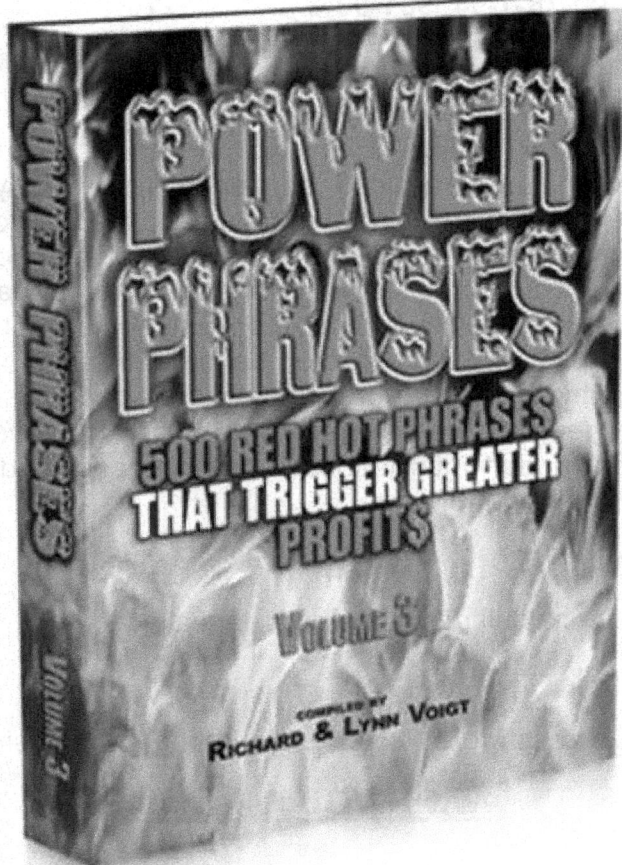

POWER PHRASES – Vol. 3
500 Power Phrases That Trigger Greater Profits

ISBN-13: 978-1-940961-03-3
ISBN-10: 1940961033

First Printing, 2013

Printed in the United States of America

To Access More Powerful Marketing Tools Visit:

www.RIVObooks.com

www.RIVOinc.com

www.WisconsinGarden.com

POWER

PHRASES

Volume 3

500 POWER PHRASES THAT TRIGGER GREATER PROFITS

-·|·-•·*”""*·•·_·|·-•**•-·|·-•·*”""”*·•-·|·-

Compiled by

Richard & Lynn Voigt
I.M. Education Specialists

Introduction:

Powerful Phrases, Headlines, Sub Headlines, Slogans, Bullet Points and Interview Sound Bites are perhaps the most powerful marketing tools mankind has ever created. They are the lifeblood behind every business venture are the ultimate secret weapon of Millionaire Marketers.

No matter whether you are introducing or promoting a brand new product, teaching a "How To" skill, building a website, or simply sending an email, using the perfect power phrase is crucial to capturing and holding eyeballs and producing greater marketing profits.

In today's world every word you use has measurable impact. Each word can produce emotional psychological buttons that trigger psychological reactions. Successful advertisers understand that using an effective power phrase is a true art form that turns "wants" into instant gratification "needs." Once artfully triggered, any niche market can instantly create more protifable conversions.

Now it's your turn to personalize this incredible collection of 500 Power Phrases in ways that instantly advance your own effective marketing skills as you create new and power phrases, slogans, presentations, bullet points, or interview sound bites that take you to the next level.

Whether starting or running a small business, writing an ad, coming up with a memorable slogan, making a major corporate presentation, bullet points, creating a video, writing a book, searching for the perfect slogan, teaching a lesson or book report, your creative use of these Power Phrases can capture more eyeballs and produce some amazing rewards quickly turning you into a Marketing Genius. Now, it's your turn to make the magic happen!

POWER PHRASES

Volume 3 – 1001 - 1500

500 Power Phrases That Trigger Greater Profits

Begin Selecting & Customizing Your Perfect Marketing Phrase

1001	Know What You Really Want
1002	Work To Zero Work
1003	Making It Instantly Available
1004	This Site Could Be Banned At Any Moment
1005	Best File Compression Around
1006	Seeking More Exposure
1007	Building Schools In The Cloud
1008	Avoid Selling Passion
1009	Simple And Powerful
1010	I Know How
1011	Have All The Success You Could Ever Want
1012	Red Hot Tip
1013	Perfect Marketing Partners
1014	The Answer We've Been Looking For
1015	When To Feel Awesome
1016	Don't Kick Yourself In The Butt Over This Mistake
1017	Why Settle For Seconds
1018	Make Feeling A Broad Adventure
1019	Killer Marketer Stalks And Plots His Moves Effectively
1020	Take A Breath And Continue
1021	What's Your Innovation Capital Worth
1022	Amazing Sneaky Trick

7

1061	Feeding The Need To Know
1062	Physical Emotional And Logical Conflicts
1063	Let's Get Into The Nitty Gritty
1064	Why I Saved My Head
1065	How Low Can You Go
1066	Limited Time Offer Don't Miss Out
1067	Will You Chop Your Video
1068	Unleash Your Inner Genie
1069	Double Your Enrollment
1070	For Those Who Can't Wait
1071	Bounce On Your Butt
1072	I Got Myself A Coach
1073	Twist Your Way To Trimmer Abs
1074	Be A Marketing Sampler
1075	How Many Of You Could Use This Now
1076	Not Just For Headlines
1077	Punch It Up Rather Than Punching Yourself
1078	This Fall's Hottest Offer
1079	Want To Advertise To Millions Legitimately
1080	Consumer Behaviors Are Changing
1081	Relax With Results
1082	Create Your Own Dream Life Style Here
1083	Facing A Long Hard Climb
1084	Most People Who See This Won't Even Try
1085	Let's Start Publishing Shift
1086	What Things Do You Power
1087	Enunciate Each Word
1088	Feast And Fun
1089	Has That Day Never Come
1090	Learn To Say It Differently
1091	Reassure Yourself You're Ready
1092	Ready For A Change
1093	Golden Goose Turns Customers Into Repeat Buyers
1094	Still Seeing Green
1095	There's Not A Lot Of Time Left
1096	Life Can Be Sweet
1097	How To Beat A Billion Dollar Company
1098	Having Inter-Operational Discord

1137	Learn To Question Everything
1138	Justify Every Penny Spent
1139	Help Your Users Get Started Right Now
1140	How To Position Your Headlines
1141	Get Out There And Test It
1142	When Buy Is Bought
1143	Don't Let People Get To You
1144	Become Their Advocate
1145	Show Up Energized
1146	It's A Worthy Divergence
1147	Extremely Easy To Do
1148	Dominate Your Own Market Before It Disappears
1149	Richest Market On Earth
1150	You're Sure To Find What You Need Right Here
1151	Million Dollar Idea
1152	Give Me A List Of Your Favorite Movies
1153	My Secret Cash Strategies And Wealth Making Methods
1154	Offer Something Extremely Unique
1155	Even A Monkey Could Get Sign Ups Using This
1156	Sustainable Development
1157	Tweaked And Optimized To Perfection
1158	It's Just Because You Don't Know Where To Start
1159	Time Sensitive Opportunity
1160	Get The Full Story Here
1161	More Automation More Income
1162	Headlines Must Speak For Themselves
1163	My Affiliate Strategy
1164	Seven Figure Income
1165	30-Day Free Trial
1166	They'll Either Opt-In Or Die
1167	Men Respond To Money
1168	A Chance To Make Awesome Money On Autopilot
1169	You'll Be Thoroughly Blown Away
1170	They're Going To Give You Superficial Answers
1171	Stranded On Your Online Raft
1172	Quality Web Promotions
1173	Ensure A Seamless Blend
1174	Never Has Advertising Been So Profitable

1212	**The Average Stick Rate Is 9-14 Months**
1213	**This Winter's Hottest Offer**
1214	**Follow Your Dreams**
1215	**Created To Run Automatically**
1216	**This Is No Longer Just Theory**
1217	**Did Yesterday Really Happen**
1218	**Time To Start Building Your List**
1219	**Talking Head Videos**
1220	**Has Your ISP Website Been Shutdown**
1221	**The Only Person To Spend Your Time On**
1222	**How To Find A Market That's Perfect For You**
1223	**Listen To It Now**
1224	**You've Got To Know Your Stuff**
1225	**Finding Old Friends**
1226	**A Truly Unique Problem With A Quick Solution**
1227	**Who's Talking About You**
1228	**Why Lose When You Can Win**
1229	**How To Find A Money-Making Niche**
1230	**Most Problems Are Due To Miscommunication**
1231	**Compel And Seduce Your Decision Makers**
1232	**Here's All That Making Money Is**
1233	**Bamboo Glasses**
1234	**My Hobby Was Collecting Money**
1235	**Stay Within Your Gesture Frame**
1236	**Who Knew What This Little Button Could Do**
1237	**You MUST Act Now**
1238	**Zero Sum Game With Clear Winners**
1239	**Get Rid Of Those Constant Set Back Excuses**
1240	**People Hate To Be Sold**
1241	**Learn From The Best And Copy Them**
1242	**Make A Commitment To Act**
1243	**Will You Be Ready For This**
1244	**That's What I Want For You**
1245	**When The Answer Is YES**
1246	**It Set The Light Bulb Off**
1247	**Stunning Pay-Offs**
1248	**Speak For Your Stomach**
1249	**Super Affiliate Strategies**

1250	Unlock The Secret To Accumulating Wealth
1251	Call Here And Receive A $10 Discount
1252	Dependable Monthly Income Generator
1253	Be Proud Of Your Product Or Service
1254	What's Your Social Media Edgerank
1255	Limping From One Crisis To Another
1256	It's Time To Make Your Choice
1257	Well Developed Goal
1258	Who Stole Your Bonus Check Today
1259	Show Me Your Skills
1260	Stimulate Your Thinking
1261	That's No Way To Make A Living
1262	Jaw Dropping Wonder
1263	Web Audio Waiting To Record Your Success Story
1264	K.I.S.S Need I Say More
1265	An Average Guy Who Knows What Works
1266	Why Are You Giving That Away For Free
1267	Results Other Got
1268	Why Customers Recommend Only Us
1269	Category Audios
1270	Unlock The Truth Behind More Traffic
1271	What Really Works Anymore
1272	From Puffery To Praise: How To Turn Hype Into Sales
1273	Opportunity Focus Time
1274	Effective Openings
1275	Deal Of The Week
1276	No Product Start With Bypass Surgery
1277	Talk Is Cheap
1278	Blistering Fast Delivery
1279	Don't Limit Your Life By Thinking What You Can Have
1280	You're Order Is On Its Way
1281	I'm Not Going To Place A Limit On Your Profits
1282	The School Of Getting It Done
1283	Just Like Telling A Story
1284	Fixing A Negative Image
1285	Category Scientific Advertising
1286	This Safelist Has Active Members Ready To See Your Ads
1287	Putting The Power Of Publishing In Your Hands

1288	The Question That Is Right In The Zone
1289	Subhead Your Links
1290	What If It's Not Engaging
1291	Unlock My Brain
1292	This Definitely Ranks Top Of The Marketing Charts
1293	Eliminate Stress And Anxiety From Your Life
1294	Stop Setting Goals To Achieve Success
1295	Marketing Landscape Changes
1296	Kickstart Your Greatest Dreams
1297	Reclaim Your Childhood
1298	Real Revenue Model
1299	Focus And Explain Your Business With Total Clarity
1300	Enjoy This In Your Car
1301	Pass The Vision
1302	Are We Really Alone Online
1303	Restore Your Focus
1304	Gravitate Toward Those Who Value Your Products
1305	Jumping From Program To Program
1306	Pay Per Action
1307	Are You Receiving Advanced Notification
1308	Take Your Game Online
1309	Don't Let Them Cut You Out Of Your Sale
1310	Online Money-Making Guide
1311	Beginner Or Veteran Who Haven't Figured It Out
1312	Why It Will Make You Wealthy
1313	Trying To Reclaim Your Image
1314	I Give Myself Goosebumps
1315	This Is Not A Get Rich Quick Scheme
1316	Are You Willing To Share Your Knowledge
1317	Let's Talk About The Marketing Of It
1318	Did You Receive My Email Or Should I Resend
1319	Define Success For Yourself
1320	Make Money Without Paypal
1321	Educated Out Of Creativity
1322	Learn From The Cloud
1323	Connecting With Real People
1324	Boost Your Energy
1325	Don't Miss This Again

14

1326	I Wanted To Send You This Sooner
1327	Bonus Baiting Affiliate Commissions On Steroids
1328	I'll Be Hooking You Up Today
1329	They're Even Giving Away Prizes
1330	How To Win The Battle
1331	One Begins Where One Is
1332	That Has To Be Sexier
1333	Awesome New Ad Site Plus Guaranteed Income
1334	You Can Never Have Too Much
1335	When Hard Work Pays Big Time
1336	Time And Resources
1337	Which Problem Do You Want To Beat
1338	Put Yourself In A Different Atmosphere
1339	The Biggest Bonus Of All
1340	Few Have A Clue
1341	Internet Marketers Hall Of Shame
1342	What Happens When You're Not Prepared
1343	Where To Do It Right
1344	Puppy Dog Licks
1345	Price Will Be Going Up
1346	Is Writing Too Tedious
1347	Milquetoast Marketing
1348	Three Tips For Finding Top Shelf Clients
1349	Website Feeling Embarrassed Lately
1350	Money Making Cravings
1351	Touching The Heart Of The Matter
1352	Different Marketing Techniques And Strategies
1353	Finding Bad Ass Products That Make Tons Of Money
1354	How Has Playing It Safe Made You Any Real Money
1355	How Do You Know When You Found The Right Solution
1356	Swipe File Examples
1357	We Want To Support Your Business
1358	Spare Time Money
1359	Looks Like You Ignored This Yesterday
1360	Don't Be Afraid To Blink
1361	We Have All You Need Here
1362	Why The Wizard Fried His Own Brain Waves Over This
1363	Who's Your Keyword Watchdog

16

1402	I'm Going To Rip You Off
1403	Turning On Your Prospects
1404	Just As They Are
1405	How To Save A Bundle
1406	A Niche Must Be Discovered Uncovered And Solved
1407	Never Miss A Beat
1408	Pushing Noodles
1409	Becoming Financially Free Requires Skill And Action
1410	No Expertise Required
1411	Combining The Best Features From Several Different Business Models
1412	Has Advertising Failed
1413	Boost Your Business
1414	Avoid These High Risk Changes
1415	Our Goal Is To Make A Sale
1416	Launch Pad For New Ads
1417	See What Inspires You
1418	6 Reasons Why You Should Upgrade Now
1419	Lost Your Way
1420	Here's The Straight Poop
1421	Harpoon Their Eyeballs
1422	Great Content Great Price Great Bargain
1423	Getting One Action
1424	Serialize Many Pieces Of Your Content
1425	Generates A Lot Of Traffic
1426	$1 For Any Four Books
1427	Connect With The Floor To Your Feet
1428	The Plague Of Denial
1429	Simple Steps Anyone Can Follow
1430	Now To The Sales Page
1431	Take Your Step Forward
1432	Never Assume Anything
1433	Just Haven't Gotten Around To It Yet
1434	Sex Sells Or At Lease Allusions Does
1435	Use Them For Good And Not For Evil
1436	Score This Touchdown
1437	Exploiting Your Voice
1438	Prices Will Decline

17

1439	Time Tested Secrets
1440	Tangible And Emotional
1441	Do Your Keywords Matter Anymore
1442	What Customers Really Want From You
1443	Are You Sabotaging Your Own Website
1444	Sure Ain't Grandpa's Way Of Doing Things
1445	You Want To Talk Money
1446	Words Fly Fast Yet Images Linger In Your Mind
1447	Stimulate Their Sense Of Curiosity
1448	Handing Power Back To You
1449	This Could Be Our Little Secret
1450	The Ultimate Image
1451	Try Link Bait To Catch Customers
1452	Amazing Affiliate Reports
1453	Is This What You Asked For
1454	The Bonus Just Got Bigger
1455	Do Not Hesitate
1456	Selling To The Senses
1457	Tap Into The Story Well
1458	Never Make Another Cold Contact
1459	Innovate Your Business Model Now For Profitability
1460	The Leading Premise Of Wealth
1461	Speechless vs. Spellbound
1462	You're In For One Helluva Ride
1463	Think About What You Really Want
1464	Breaking Down Every Facet
1465	Creating A Road Map For Success
1466	Fast Action Bonuses
1467	Benefit From My Marketing Mistakes
1468	The Dirty Little Secret Worth Stealing
1469	Inside The Members Area
1470	The Real Shift In Marketing
1471	Outdrive Your Competitors
1472	Look Slim Trim And Fit
1473	Overly Shiny Lipstick Distracts
1474	Do A Price Check
1475	Being Over Promised
1476	Why Do We Need To Learn This

1477	You Can See The Whites Of Their Teeth
1478	Tired Of Being Bamboozled
1479	Short Sales Pages
1480	How To Profit From Seismic Changes
1481	A Vicious Circle Of Decline
1482	Good Stuff Is Becoming More Infrequent
1483	Reduce The Cost Of Marketing Experiments
1484	Do You Have Performance Chops
1485	The Best Kept Healing Secrets In The World
1486	Pro Active Phone Update Service
1487	Copy And Paste Then Money Flows
1488	Perfect For Sleeping
1489	Your Price For Getting Access To This Killer Program
1490	Sick Of Doing Everything Yourself
1491	No Fast Hand Movement
1492	Which Ones Would You Like Now
1493	Borrow Credibility
1494	Approved By Industry Leaders
1495	Need A Leash
1496	Outsourcing Can Be Tempting
1497	Alignment And Proximity
1498	Earn Big Bucks Online
1499	Verify Their Existence
1500	Puts You In Control

Lynn and I hope that this "Think Tank" volume series of 500 Hot Phrases will helped you clearly paint your dreams, sell your ideas, and market your messages, propelling each of your ideas and projects toward incredible success. Watch for our next Volume!

We truly wish you the very best and look forward to hearing your success stories.

Concluding Thoughts:

19

Ever success is built upon a preparing a strong foundation, having a clear vision, and taking positive action each and every day. If you've been searching for a new lifestyle, then you'll find this book directive and inspirational. You can open it to any page and let that page help you rethink possibilities, consider new ideas, open new opportunities, and ultimately experience a more successful and fulfilling lifestyle.

Every problem has a solution! Regardless of your current situation or circumstance, know that you have the power and responsibility to redirect your life in any direction you choose. Simply start thinking about and research the kind of lifestyle that truly appeals to your heart. Begin your new journey by learning everything you can about your chosen subject. When you make that commitment, you'll open more unexpected doors to unique opportunities than imagined.

"Creative Thought Is The Only Reality
Everything Else Is Merely The By-Product Of That Thought."
- Walter Russell

So why not start thinking **BIGGER? It won't cost you any more.** It all starts by never allowing your current life's situation, environment, or so-called friends to limit your path to a happier, healthier, and successful life. After all, whose life is this?

Make a decision to focus on learning something new each and every day. Begin attracting your ideal lifestyle by doing something you love and enjoy. As difficult as it may be, don't allow money to limit your dreams. Focus on the kind of thoughts that make you feel good. Once you learn how to control your focus, you'll have a great chance to see your dreams take shape. You've finally learn to harness the power you always had within, a Universal Energy stream that flows 365/24/7 in any direction your project your thoughts, Good or Bad. Want proof? The thoughts you currently believe and project reflect the life you're currently living. Therefore, if your life isn't happening, change your thoughts, and change your life. It's something only you can hold, visualize, and project, living your dream come true.

Find yourself a mentor and spend more time with people who truly appreciate, support, and foster your dreams. Life may be short, but the thoughts we hold can make our life wider and more fulfilling.

About The Authors:

20

Richard and Lynn develop creative strategies that paint dreams, sell ideas, & market messages   Together, they present a unique team-approach, working side-by-side, helping clients pursue their passions while sharing their skills and diverse expertise as authors, artists, inventors, entrepreneurs, & Internet marketing education specialists.

Teaching by example, they mentor proven self-publishing services, graphic design, video production, domain acquisition, and marketing research of behalf of their company, RIVO Inc – RIVO Marketing, since 1997. They've created & produced hundreds of videos, self-published dozens of books on a wide variety of topics and created thousands of original works of fine art, while refining their Internet Marketing techniques, mentoring programs, and related business website development.

Their mission is to continually uncover new products and services, test new strategies, and network useful solutions with off and online entrepreneurs, small business owners, writers, local artists, models, teachers, students, and marketing professionals.

Their goal is to help clients create an action plan that discovers and connects the missing pieces of the success puzzle. The goals they foster create multiple streams of income for today's volatile economic climate. Their motto is: "Do the work once and allow the work to create additional streams of income for a lifetime."

Feel free to contact them if you have questions or would like to tap into their talents and expertise. They appreciate your feedback and look forward to hearing your success stories.

Contact:
Richard & Lynn Voigt - RIVO
I. M. Education Specialists

RIVO INC - RIVO Marketing
13720 West Keefe Avenue
Brookfield, Wisconsin 53005 – USA
Email: support@RIVOinc.com
Website: www.RIVObooks.com
Website: www.WisconsinGarden.com

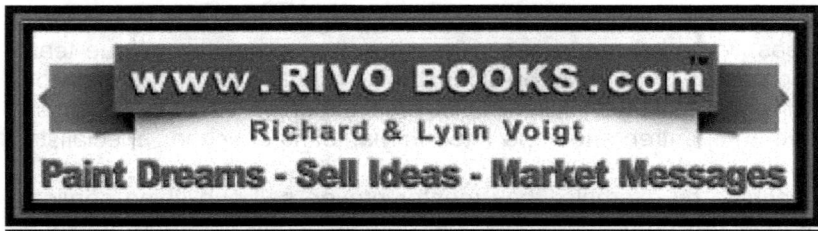

Visit Lynn's Garden: www.WisconsinGarden.com
view hundreds of great garden video blogs Tips

See Richard's Unique Artwork: www.RIVOart.com
view over 3,000 original Fine-Art compositions

Our Book Titles Now Available On Amazon:

THE GOLDEN VAULT OF MOTIVATIONAL QUOTATIONS
Words of Wisdom from The Greatest Minds & Leaders

BABY NAME .ME - 21,400 Names & Nicknames
For Family, Friends, Pets, Natural & Man-Objects

DOODLE DESIGNS Volumes 1-3
For Professionals & Kids Of All Ages
DOODLE DESIGNS – Vol. 1
DOODLE DESIGNS – Vol. 2
DOODLE DESIGNS Coloring Book Vol. 3

Work MORE Accomplish LESS Get FIRED!

ACTION HEADLINES That Drive Emotions – Volumes 1- 6
 Paint Dreams, Sell Ideas & Market Your Message
Action Headlines That Drive Emotions Vol. 1
Action Headlines That Drive Emotions Vol. 2
Action Headlines That Drive Emotions Vol. 3
Action Headlines That Drive Emotions Vol. 4
Action Headlines That Drive Emotions Vol. 5
Action Headlines That Drive Emotions Vol. 6

IDIOMS – IDIOMS - IDIOMS
6,450 Popular Expressions That Put Words In Your Mouth

The CLICHÉ BIBLE - 8,400 Clichés For Sports Fanatics
& Lovers Of Popular Expressions

MORE THAN WORDS
5000+ Marketing Phrases That Sell

HYPNOTIC PHRASING
WARNING-This Book Teaches You How To Grab Eyeballs

22

YOUR RIGHT TO WEALTH
Becoming Wealthy Isn't Hard When You Know How

WI GARDEN – Let's Get Dirty
Our Wisconsin Garden Guide Promoting Delicious, Healthier Home-Grown Fresh Food, With Tools, Tips, & Ideas That Inspire Gardeners!

MONETIZE YOUR SOCIAL LIFE
Earn Extra Income While Having Fun Online

BABY NAMES
21,400 Unique Baby Names & Nicknames

FUNNY HEADLINES vol. 1
3,500 Outrageous Silly Brain Toots

FUNNY HEADLINES vol. 2
3,500 Outrageous Silly Brain Toots

JOBS
10,240 Career Paths That Can Change Your Life!

MONEY WORDS
Powerful Phrases That Million Dollar Copywriters Use To Make Piles Of Cash On Demand!

GARDEN QUOTATIONS
400 Garden Quotes From The Earth To Your Soul

HEADLINE STARTERS
175,000 Words That Paint Dreams, Sell Ideas, And Market Your Message

BABY NAMES
25,350 Baby Names & Nicknames For Your Family Friends & Pets
    697 pages 7,000 Names with Origin & Meaning plus Top 100 Names, And 2,000 Most Popular Names

CURIOUS WORDS
15,800 Words That Expand Your Mind And Change Your Life

INSPIRING THOUGHTS
That Inspire Happiness, Success & A Clearer Understanding Of Life

MARKETING EYEBALLS
100 Ideas That Can Add Unlimited Subscribers To Your Lists

SECOND OF FIVE

My Early Years- From Birth To High School

POWER PHRASES – Individual Volumes 1 - 10
500 Power Phrases That Trigger Greater Profits

POWER PHRASES Pro Edition – Volumes 1-10 (Complete Series)
5000 Power Phrases That Trigger Greater Profits

COMING SOON! – BE THE FIRST TO GRAB YOUR PRO COPY

POWER PHRASES Pro Edition Volumes 1-10 (Complete Series)
5000 Power Phrases That Trigger Greater Profits

What do Marketing Millionaires know that you don't? They know how to pull money out of thin air by using their secret language of Power Phrases.

This Pro Edition of 5000 Red Hot Power Phrases not only saves you time and money but will help jump-start your creative brain in ways you may have never considered. Simply open this amazing collection to any page and find your perfect power phrase. All it may take is simply adding or replacing ONE word. It's simple, quick, and easy!

1. **Want to create more powerful profitable campaign offers?**
2. **Thinking of revitalizing a more professional business identity?**
3. **Want to update old product or service media advertisements?**
4. **Searching for fresh ideas that could improve sales and profits?**
5. **Looking for brand new ways to create stronger media sales copy?**
6. **Ready to use millionaire strategies advancing you to the next level?**

5000 POWER PHRASES is exclusively for professional Internet Marketers, authors,advertisers, executives, business owners, TV & radio reporters, entrepreneurs, administrators, managers, supervisors, teachers and students who want to find and access unique phrases for marketing slogans, presentation bullet points, and interview sound bites that powerfully paint dreams, sell ideas, and market your message.

Stop wasting valuable time, money, and energy racking your brain for new ideas. Create more profitable power phrase marketing campaigns for all your products, services, slogans, bullet points, and interview sound bites that finally grab and hold people's attention and trigger greater profits?

You now have a very powerful and professional marketing tool in your hand. We are confident that you know how to use it wisely in order to maximize the potential of all your marketing campaigns! Lynn and I **Thank You** for your support and purchase.

CLAIM 500 MORE POWER PHRASES!

Thank you for purchasing this eBook and in doing so we would like to send you **500 More Red Hot Power Phrases for FREE!**

When you post a **positive review of this Book on Amazon Books** under this title you'll receive an additional **500 POWER PHRASES.** Your review may also be sent directly to us.

Your request must be received within 30-days of purchase. Once your positive Book review is posted and verified, simply email the following to **(500@RIVOinc.com)**:

1. Full Name of Purchaser
2. Email address
3. Paypal Invoice Number
4. Copy of your posted Book Review*

Once we receive the above, we'll send you 500 Power Phrases **(PDF)** emailed to the address you provided.

Visit: www.RIVObooks.com for additional volumes as they become available including the Pro Edition of 5000 Red Hot Power Phrases that say what you mean to say and trigger greater profits.

Lynn and I look forward to your written comments and suggestions as we love hearing from each of our readers.

Richard & Lynn Voigt
RIVO Inc – RIVO Marketing
13720 West Keefe Avenue
Brookfield, Wisconsin 53005 USA
Telephone: (262) 783-5335
www.RIVObooks.com

P. S. If you love gardening, catch us on www.WisconsinGarden.com

*NOTE: This offer is valid providing it does not violate the terms of service of the entity with whom you made this purchase. Duplicate or incomplete entries will also not be eligible and this offer is limited to one request per email address. All eligible review submissions become the property of RIVO Inc - RIVO Marketing – RIVO books and may be used as promotional testimonials ads on RIVO Inc websites. This offer may be withdrawn at any time without prior written notice.